DEDICATION

Thank you first to my family, and to Sacramento for giving me a life that has exceeded my dreams! Also thank you to my first boss, John Clay, who taught me that a broadcast market is first and foremost a community, and to give back to that community relentlessly. He also helped me edit this book and likely corrected many misspelled words, such as "relentlessly."

100 THINGS TO DO IN SACRAMENTO BEFORE YOU DIE

2nd Edition

HARLOW'S
RESTAURANT & NIGHTCLUB
500 DAYS DARK
REOPENING 8·12
SEE YOU SOON
SACRAMENTO
THE
STARLET
ROOM

100 THINGS TO DO IN SACRAMENTO BEFORE YOU DIE

2nd Edition

MARK S. ALLEN

Reedy Press
PO Box 5131
St. Louis, MO 63139, USA
www.reedypress.com

Library of Congress Control Number: 2019956364

ISBN: 9781681062648

Design by Jill Halpin

Photos by author unless otherwise noted.

Printed in the United States of America
21 22 23 24 25   5 4 3 2 1

CONTENTS

Music and Entertainment

Sports and Recreation

Culture and History

PREFACE

This book is very special to me, even more so than the first edition, largely because it's a celebration of survival. The businesses within these pages went through the 2020–2021 pandemic, and despite the barrage of obstacles and the countless shape shifting hurdles, they made it. Not only did they make it, but in many ways they grew stronger.

I moved to Sacramento from Southern California, and very quickly fell in love with the people, the places, and the vibe. When I first arrived, the standard, flippant response to, "What is there to do in Sacramento?" was, "One, go to San Francisco. Two, go to Tahoe" etc. However, in this millennium, Sacramento has evolved into a history-filled, culturally explosive, world-class destination, and one of California's must-visit places. Time magazine wrote the headline, "Sacramento Is the Most Integrated and Culturally Diverse City in America." And you are about to find out why.

I've now logged over 30,000 hours of local TV time here, much of that shining light on local businesses. I've also produced six feature films using locations within the Sacramento area. To each and every owner and staff member who had to get out of bed at 4 a.m. for one of my 5 a.m. broadcasts, I say thank you! And to any of the locations who allowed our Hollywood crews to invade your space for a time, thanks to you as well. Just know that those moments were probably why you were at the top of my mind when I wrote this book.

Perhaps you were given this book as a Welcome Wagon gift, or maybe you're a local who needs a reminder of all the great things you've been meaning to do. Either way, I think it will come in handy. I've tried to balance between expensive and free, and have taken a TMZ approach: Sacramento proper gets first billing, but anything exceptional within a thirty-mile zone from city center was also considered.

Narrowing, not expanding, the list was the hardest part. Next door to almost every awesome place you find in these pages is an equally awesome place that I had to cut to get the list down to just one hundred. Have fun, and be sure to join other readers on Facebook @100ThingsSac to report your discoveries! Enjoy!

ACKNOWLEDGMENTS

For helping to make this book possible:

Thank you to the great people and businesses of Sacramento and surrounding communities for telling me about their favorite places, and for tolerating my antics and adventures on and off screen for more than 35 years.

Thanks to my remarkable family for putting up with our crazy schedule and life. I take joy every day knowing that they're out there discovering new things to do and adding chapters each day to their life books.

Thanks to my mentor and best friend John Clay for his painstaking editing of this book.

And big thanks to Jill Eccher, Josh Stevens, Barbara Northcott, and everyone at Reedy Press for their immense patience in putting this edition together.

BAR

FOOD AND DRINK

1

EAT *IN* THE KITCHEN

Imagine your friend is one of the world's best chefs, his friend is one of Northern California's leading sommeliers, they're super friendly and funny, and they invite you over for wine tasting and a four-hour feast! That's what it's like at the Kitchen, where the food is amazing and plentiful, and you'll want for nothing. It's a bit pricey, about two hundred dollars per person, but this is a special occasion, right? I put it first because if you make reservations now, you may get to this by the time you finish the others on the list (seriously, plan at least five months ahead). This was my first meal when I moved to Northern California, as a treat from my new employer; my next meal was two-for-ninety-nine-cents tacos. Back to you—do this. It is a bucket-list-worthy foodgasm!

2225 Hurley Way, 916-568-7171
thekitchenrestaurant.com

The menu is prix-fixe, and you'll get your money's worth, but add on the wine pairing; you'll save bucks. Also get ready to be tempted to sample some very, very expensive sakes and whiskeys. If you so indulge, do.

2

TRY
THE NEW iTACO AT CHANDO'S

Let me explain: I've never met a taco I didn't like. However, Chando's Tacos are not only the absolute best street tacos I have ever experienced, but they are also the only street tacos created by a former Apple executive. Lisandro "Chando" Madrigal left the iPhone mothership and, within six years, had his NorCal taco empire established. Chando discovered his love of tacos on a family trip to Mexico when he was a kid, where beneath the neon lights and busy streets in Tijuana, he saw white taco carts on nearly every corner. Though there are several versions of this taco-stand-turned-sit-down (including the new ten-thousand-square-foot restaurant & operations center in West Sacramento), you really should head to the one that started it all.

863 Arden Way, 916-641-8226
chandostacos.com

3

LIVE
THE AMERICAN DREAM (ROLL)

You'll find it at Mikuni, and if you are lucky, your life will be transformed as you meet owner & chef Taro Arai. At the tender age of eleven, Taro saved $6,000 from his paper route to move his family from Japan to Sacramento, where not long after, they created this gem. The rolls are all original and amazing. The fusion sushi is East meets West Coast meets East Coast meets Taro. Case in point: the 24k roll contains real twenty-four-karat gold and is aptly priced. There are plenty of locations around the Sacramento area, and you can enjoy Mikuni at a Kings game in Golden 1 Center. Check the website for special events and classes, including public or private sushiology lessons.

1530 J St., 916-447-2112
mikunisushi.com

4

INDULGE
IN MIDNIGHT MILKSHAKES

Rick's Dessert Diner is great at all hours, but even better after spilling out of a show, concert, or club downtown. Award-winning milkshakes, and cakes, and pies come with a price: you will stand in a line with customers "anxious to get their carb on," but otherwise very nice people just like you. Rick's Dessert Diner has more than 285 varieties of European and American desserts, all made fresh daily from scratch, using generations-old recipes originating in France, Italy, Germany, Sweden, Switzerland, and even early America. And Rick's custom cakes for birthdays, anniversaries, weddings, and showers are works of art. I challenge you to peruse the menu without your mouth watering. Voted "Best of Sacramento" for dessert every year since 1986!

2401 J St., 916-444-0969
ricksdessertdiner.com

ENJOY A BUSHTIT
AT DARLING AVIARY

Fortunately you already know that an aviary is a bird sanctuary, and that certainly we *must* be talking about birds, so you weren't instantly offended! Indeed that's the name of one of the best burgers on the planet! In fact all the burgers and sandwiches on the menu at Darling Aviary have fancy bird names. Plus you may sip some cocktails, wine, or beer while you enjoy some of the best elevated views of Sacramento in this lofty restaurant lounge. My job takes me around the globe to interview celebrities, and I've had the privilege of eating at some of the finest restaurants with spectacular views. From that perspective, I can tell you with complete confidence that Darling Aviary offers the best views overlooking Sacramento.

712 K St., 916-758-5715
darlingaviary.com

6

EAT VIP
AT THE FIREHOUSE

Every city has "that" restaurant, expensive and historic, where old money, new money, and people celebrating special occasions all converge. The Firehouse is just that in Sacramento. Ronald Reagan had his inaugural dinner here, and The Firehouse has hosted every California governor since. Paul McCartney and a roster of A-listers far too long for this book have chosen this venue for their Sacramento dining. Try to talk your waiter into a tour of the wine cellar, where Andy Warhol once perused the twenty thousand bottles to choose from while eating a cheeseburger with Mario the sommelier!

1112 Second St., 916-442-4772
firehouseoldsac.com

TIP

A quirky thing I love about The Firehouse—Sacramento's most elegant and luxurious dining establishment—is that when you're done for the evening and wander out its back courtyard, you walk directly into Sacramento's most beloved dive bar, aptly named "The Back Door."

CELEBRATE
OCTOBERFEST 365

But at Der Biergarten, they'll ask you to spell it "Oktoberfest." Der Biergarten is a beer lover's dream come true. It's authentically German, with an extensive beer selection and a light German food menu, including thirty-two beers on draft and sausages brought in fresh from Sacramento's number-one German butcher. Even its tables were shipped to Sacramento from relatives in Germany, and you will be seated in a communal atmosphere, sipping great German beer from half- and full-liter steins. The experience is one hundred percent outdoors, so you can enjoy the great Sacramento weather by day and the stars by night. Make sure you plan to stay a while, and plan a safe ride home. While you came to eat and drink, you'll likely be challenged to a game of cornhole, foosball, or ping-pong. Lederhosen are optional, although I've never really seen any here.

2332 K St., 916-346-4572
beergardensacramento.com

SACRAMENTO'S MICROBREWS ABOUND! HERE ARE THE MUST-SIPS

Ruhstaller

Founded by Captain Frank Ruhstaller, "California's premier pioneer brewer," more than 130 years ago. The good captain grew the finest hops and barley by partnering with California farmers.

726 K St., 916-447-1881
ruhstallerbeer.com

Oak Park Brewing Company

Set in a lovely ninety-year-old building that makes you feel like you're on a luxurious rustic ship—and they have extraordinary beer! There are usually seven beers on tap, and each one always seems to be from a different planet than the one beside it. The British and Belgian ales have often been described as having a "West Coast kick," and the IPAs are known for being aromatic and hoppy, with a smooth malt finish.

3514 Broadway, 916-389-0726
opbrewco.com

TIP

Come here to buy a "growler" and to find out what that actually is!

Drake's BARN

Set along the river in West Sacramento's Bridge District, Drake's BARN is a two-acre entertainment and beer destination. Includes PizzaSmith restaurant, food trucks, a four-hundred-seat beer garden and bar, and fire pits, plus live music and DJs on three stages and a large open meadow with beach chairs and lawn games. With more than 25 styles of brewed deliciousness, this is the place where you just may find your perfect brew!

985 Riverfront St., West Sacramento, 510-423-0971
drinkdrakes.com

8

YO, MOFO!

When the food truck explosion was sweeping the nation, Sacramento's finest trucks gathered for a cooperative summit, and SactoMoFo (Sacramento Mobile Food Events) was born! Drewski's Hot Rod Kitchen is uniquely Sacramento, with the most amazing pulled pork sandwiches I've had anywhere in the world. Bacon Mania serves dishes that are all about the bacon, including crisps, sandwiches, fries, and mac & cheese. Its Nacho Truck has taken cheese on chips to an art form; just remember the slogan—"It's Nacho Truck . . . It's Mine!" SactoMoFo's list is long and proud. Catch the list for these and more than thirty other once-in-a-lifetime-experience food trucks at its site; check for locations and dates.

sactomofo.com

9

PINCH A TAIL
AND SUCK A HEAD AT CRAWDADS ON THE RIVER

That is a perfectly family-friendly play-by-play tutorial on how to eat crayfish, and that's exactly what's on the menu at Crawdads on the River. Sacramento is a river city, after all, and many a worthy eatery lines the banks. However, this one will put you on the river and into the action. Adam Pechal and Paul Caravelli, both from ABC's *The Taste*, teamed up to resurrect this floating dining, drinking party barge-meets-refined living. Make reservations to be outside on a nice day, and Louisiana-inspired anything on the menu will meet high expectations. Make friends with the people next to you who own the million-dollar yacht they've just docked, and your night may get more interesting!

1375 Garden Hwy., 916-929-2268
saccrawdads.com

10

TRY FOX AND GOOSE
FOR BREAKFAST

Neither is on the menu here at the historic Fox and Goose Public House, but now that I have your attention, *do not miss this place*! It was established in 1975, but the bones of the building date back to 1913, and it is a descendant of the original Fox and Goose in West Yorkshire, England, that has been open for more than two hundred years. It's a rare day that you're not dining next to someone from the United Kingdom, as subjects of the Queen are drawn here for a taste of home. While the English breakfasts are authentic, everything on the menu excels. The restaurant mixes coffee drinks and cocktails with equal fervor, and it's typically "pint o'clock" at any hour. Enjoy live music on weekends and some weeknights; the line can get long, but it's worth the wait.

1001 R St., 916-443-8825
foxandgoose.com

TIKI
NOT TACKY!

Imagine for a moment the coolest throwback to the 1950s tiki bar that you've seen only in the movies. Step out of the glare of the city and into a different place and time: the tiki-inspired tropical paradise that is the Jungle Bird! It's named after a 1970s drink from the Kuala Lumpur Hilton Hotel, and you'll be surrounded by decor that includes palm trees, tropical birds, bamboo lanterns, and huge totems. Tropical drinks like you've never tasted them, including 1930s & '40s throwbacks, alongside modern concoctions. And all of them are served in beautifully created glasses and mugs that you'll want to steal (but don't do that or they'll ding your credit card). Some customers drop in for just the food, including tasty pupu platters and other authentic, tasty island cuisine. The Jungle Bird will become your new favorite destination!

2516 J St., 916-476-3280
thejunglebird.com

12

FINAL DESTINATION:
HO HOS

Let me explain. Sacramento's RT (Regional Transit) light rail is one of the most efficient public transportation systems of its size in the nation, and even more popular since the Golden 1 Center made it the best way to get in and out of downtown. So now that you're using it, take advantage of its path to one of the most amazing bakery cafés you'll ever know. Take the light rail to Folsom, stay on to the very last stop, and it will drop you right at Karen's Bakery. Be prepared for a line wrapped around the block on weekends, but the wait will be well worth it.

Everything baked is exceptional, and you'll find artisan touches in every item on the breakfast and lunch menus. Be sure to save room for dessert, and I highly recommend the handcrafted Ho Hos . . . they're the best I've ever had. A disclaimer: they're the only handcrafted Ho Hos I've ever had. But regardless, I dream of them often now. What else? The Ho Hos! You just gotta try one yourself . . . dipped in chocolate ganache, with creamy rum filling. They actually are intoxicating; it's a good thing you're not driving.

705 Gold Lake Dr., Folsom, 916-985-2665
karensbakery.com

13

SQUEEZE IN
TO SQUEEZE BURGER

Long before Guy Fieri did the same on *Diners, Drive-Ins and Dives*, this godsend to the craft burger scene had a crowd from open to close. Although several other Squeeze Burger locations have opened, you may want to journey to the original to say that you did. It's a bit on the small side, best described as half a shack. And you will, no matter your girth, find yourself squeezing in to find your fit at the bar or a table. Get ready for the best cheeseburger you've ever had: order the Squeezeburger with cheese, and you'll thank me later. The cheese will ooze out onto the grill and be crisped upon delivery. The Midtown, Roseville, and other locations also have ample non-squeeze room, but the same culinary burger technology is in play.

5301 Power Inn Rd., 916-386-8599
squeezeburger.com

14

PARADISE PICNIC

There are several great spots to picnic throughout the Sacramento area, but I've picked one because you're running out of time. Selland's Market Café was created by Randall Selland, who knows a thing or two about great food; he has opened and maintains several award-winning restaurants in the region. Stop at Selland's to pick up supplies to create your own picnic, or get its pre-made picnic components for a perfect meal. I lived in NYC and discovered the internationally famous Dean & DeLuca. But Selland's is its equal and perhaps ups it in the organic, sustainable, farm-fresh way. Now that you're picnicked up, head to Paradise Beach, only one-quarter mile away, and have the best beach dining experience in town. There are three Selland's to choose from, but only this one fits the masterful picnic plan.

5340 H St., 916-736-3333
sellands.com

Paradise Beach, 5211 Carlson Dr.

DINE
ON A BRIDGE

Sacramento is officially the nation's farm-to-fork capital, and the best way to experience local food from local farms is also the hardest ticket in town to get. Once a year, our own "Golden Gate Bridge," the Tower Bridge (to West Sacramento), is closed to traffic and transformed into the Tower Bridge Gala Dinner, part of the Farm-to-Fork Taste of Summer festivities. This family-style feast features the most award-winning food and wine in the region, all prepared by local chefs, offering locally grown and artisanally prepared ingredients. You almost have to know someone, or know someone who knows someone, to get in. And if you do manage to get a pair of tickets to this extravaganza, because we now know each other (by virtue of you buying this book), I'll gladly accept your invitation to be your "plus one!" Go to the website now in hopes of getting on the list for next year . . . tickets go that fast.

Sacramento Tower Bridge, 916-808-7777
farmtofork.com

16

HAVE A 50-50
AT GUNTHER'S

Little has changed since Gunther's opened way back in 1940. Their mouth-watering ice creams are still made fresh and with the original old-school recipes. The shop also makes one hundred fruit freezes, and before you become room temperature you *must* try the 50-50 Fruit Freeze. It's a scoop of vanilla on top of the fruit freeze of your choice. As it melts, the flavors comingle into perfection. Enjoy slowly to savor the flavors—and so you don't get an ice cream headache! Full disclosure: I was torn between Gunther's and its cross-town rival, Leatherby's Family Creamery, but couldn't include both without expanding to 101 entries. I had to pick one, and Gunther's ended up being chosen by alphabetical order in the editing process. So now you know how, as the saying goes, "the sausage is made." Or should I say "how the cream is churned!"

2801 Franklin Blvd., 916-457-6646
gunthersicecream.com

SACRAMENTO HAS A LONG TRADITION OF FINE FAMILY CREAMERIES WAITING TO FREEZE YOUR BRAIN. HERE ARE TWO MORE.

Leatherby's Family Creamery

Family-run for years, throw a maraschino cherry and you'll likely hit a Leatherby in any of its three locations. Come for the sundaes, but the crab sandwich is shockingly amazing for an ice cream place!

2333 Arden Way, 916-920-8382
leatherbys.net

Vic's Ice Cream

Also a blast from the past straight out of 1947 (the year it opened), with vintage decor and vintage comfort menu. Besides ice cream, try the wonderful sandwiches, cakes, pies, and bonbons.

3199 Riverside Blvd., 916-448-0892
vicsicecream.com

17

BE A SULTAN
AT CASABLANCA

Even if you don't order the Sultan Feast at Casablanca Moroccan Restaurant (but I suggest that you do—after all this is a bucket list), you will feel like royalty! Mourhit Drissi is the owner and will make you family during your first moments here. He will help guide you through the intricacies of the meal you're about to enjoy, all still cooked from ancient traditions passed down through his family. And Mourhit will enhance the experience with anecdotal references to each dish's Moroccan origin. The atmosphere is awesome and so much fun for big groups. You'll sit on cushions and eat almost everything with only your hands. Be warned: it's located in a less-than-attractive strip mall, ugly even by strip mall standards; however, inside, Casablanca equals Xanadu!

3516 Fair Oaks Blvd., 916-979-1160

TIP

If your party wants alcohol for celebrating, Casablanca doesn't offer anything on the menu. However, there is no corkage fee, and since there is a liquor store next door, suddenly the strip mall thing isn't so bad.

18

LOSE YOURSELF
IN THE COACHELLA OF FOOD AND BEVERAGE

Part of the annual Farm-to-Fork Taste of Summer festivities is the Farm-to-Fork Festival, a one-day event that takes over ten blocks of downtown Sacramento's Capitol Mall. An aerial photograph of the miles of people leading to the Capitol looks like an inaugural celebration is taking place! Designed to showcase and celebrate where our food and drinks come from, the Farm-to-Fork Festival brings us face to face with the people who are feeding our region and the world. This free festival boasts a delicious selection of farm-to-fork offerings that are produced and available in the Sacramento region. You'll find food, wine, and beer from regional eateries and purveyors, as well as live music, five live cooking demonstration stages, a kids' zone, interactive booths from local grocers, farms, ranches, and more!

Sacramento Capitol Mall, 916-808-7777
farmtofork.com

PICNIC UNDERGROUND

Sorry to "Sacramento's best-kept secret," but I'm putting it in the book. The Underground Tasting Room presents quite possibly one of the most romantic and charming nights you can find in this town, especially at this price point. You'll travel down steps underground to the original street level of Sacramento and be surrounded by bottles emblazoned with logos of Twisted Twig and Rendez-vous wineries, among others. You'll lounge at bistro-style tables in the brick courtyard, enjoying an atmosphere reminiscent of quaint rural towns in France. Cheese plates, succulent chocolates, and more complement the tastings and/or stand on their own. You need to do this!

900 Second St., Original Level, 916-444-2349
theundergroundtastingroom.com

20

UP YOUR MOXIE

Think NYC's Little Italy meets California fresh, and that's Moxie. How often do you see this on a menu: "At Moxie, you get what you want. If it's in the building, or nearby, we will prepare it!" And they mean it. Notice the Cary Grant photo on the wall in this dimly lit, deeper-than-wide room. Perhaps you *are* in NYC! Adam, the owner, will greet you when you enter and will take you every step of the way to make sure your night is special. If he senses you want to be alone, he'll give you room. If you're social, he may sit, open a bottle of wine and share it with you. "Special" is an understatement when describing this place. Moxie is a must. There are more daily specials than there are regular items on the menu.

2028 H St., 916-443-7585

21

HAVE A MOJITO
WITH A MERMAID AT DIVE BAR

Although I've traveled around the world, I've never seen anything quite like this. At Dive Bar, a giant overhead aquarium runs the entire length of the bar. And in that aquarium . . . *Mermaids! Real mermaids!* OK, they might as well be real mermaids. Performance artists, wearing the most convincing Hollywood special effects prosthetic tails, free dive nightly and mermaid about as you sip and mingle. We took turns timing the mermaids, convinced that some of them might be the real deal because humans can't hold their breath that long. Despite the name Dive Bar, it offers quality drinks and ambiance, and occasional live music on the weekends. Regardless, you're here for the mermaids. A truly unique must-see!

1016 K St.
divebarsacramento.com

22

PATIO IT
AT PARAGARY'S

The moment you enter this open-air courtyard, you'll know you're in the right place for a special time. This bistro's airy environment opens up to a renowned patio where you can dine surrounded by waterfalls, sixty-year-old olive trees, and a giant fireplace. Founded by the late Randy Paragary, a Sacramento restaurant pioneer and my friend, he was among the few who could claim early rights to the trademark of "California cuisine." Paragary's is tried and true—and quite special for any time. If this is your first time or only time in California, after eating here you'll know you've had signature dishes at their best.

1401 Twenty-Eighth St., 916-457-5737
paragarys.com/paragarys-midtown

TIP

Not so coincidentally, Paragary's is a very convenient short walk from the Sutter Fort Hotel, also created by Randy Paragary.

23

Y'ALL SET A SPELL
ON THE PORCH

You may be in California, but drop by the Porch and you'll think you are in the South! Kick back and forget about the worries of everyday life while you experience Southern hospitality and charm, and feed your body and soul an honest-to-goodness home-cooked meal. The Porch's unique approach to authentic Southern dishes uses the finest local, seasonal, and organic ingredients to create meals from scratch, inspired by Lowcountry, Cajun, Creole, and other traditions. Local sources are used for fruits, veggies, and grains, as well as heritage breeds of pork, grass-fed beef, organic farmed seafood, and free-range chicken. Come sit a spell at the Porch, and y'all come back now, ya hear?

1815 K St., 916-444-2423
theporchrestaurantandbar.com

24

TAKE SHELTER
IN THE FORT!

The latest addition to the Capital City's hotel scene is the hip and lit, but remarkably comfortable, Fort Sutter Hotel and its built-in watering hole, The Four Palms. It is a quintessential neighborhood bar, buzzing with energy while providing the perfect scene for a post-work drink with colleagues or a gathering before a show at the B Street Theatre, right next door. The menu is self-described as approachable, featuring Cafe Bernardo favorites alongside bar exclusive dishes, an impressive selection of Northern California wines, craft beers, and artisanal signature cocktails.

1308 28th St., 916-603-2301
fortsutterhotel.com

TIP

If you are staying in this hotel, and want to step out for a late late-night bite, just around the corner is Ink Eats & Drinks—absolutely the most gourmet midnight snack you'll find in Northern California!

EAT AT CALIFORNIA'S OTHER LEGISLATIVE HOUSE

Way back in 1939, Frank Fat turned a former speakeasy into what would become the kitchen table of some of the most prominent lawmakers in America. The California State Capitol is only a block away, and Frank Fat's restaurant is where landmark bills were and continue to be negotiated over friendly meals and napkin deals by hungry legislators. Frank Fat's features traditional but elevated Chinese food, with recipes originating in Beijing, Szechuan, Guangdong, and Shanghai, as well as Hong Kong. But a strong hint of its speakeasy roots remains, with American dishes available as well. Glance around during your meal, and if anyone looks like a politician here, they probably are. Be sure to discreetly eavesdrop to hear tomorrow's news!

806 L St., 916-442-7092
frankfats.com

26

GO
TO COFFEE CHURCH

At Temple Coffee Roasters, you can walk in and order the best coffee or espresso drink you've ever had, or you can actually learn the art of coffee roasting and extracting in one of the many classes the company offers. It sounds intimidating, but it's actually fascinating and infinitely more fun than you'd expect. The syllabus says, "Covers the fundamental variables that affect coffee extraction quality including coffee-to-water ratio, agitation and more!" You'll leave enlightened, and you will be the coffee master of your domain. Multiple locations: Midtown is my favorite.

2829 S St., 916-454-1272
templecoffee.com

TIP

While you're there, look down. More than $20,000 worth of pennies are laminated and used as the flooring. Why? At the time of this printing, that remains a mystery. Maybe we'll know by the 3rd edition!

27

JOIN
THE GRANGE

Or don't. I just needed a headline! The Grange was a farmers' association organized in 1867, and this restaurant of the same name might as well have been its headquarters. Much has been said of Sacramento being the genesis of "farm to fork," and no executive chef has embraced the concept more than Oliver Ridgeway at Grange. I challenge any chef anywhere in the world to produce a better pork chop. When I asked how they're prepared, I was told, "It's brined in apple cider, vinegar, cloves, cinnamon, chili flakes, and whole oranges. The meat, submerged and chilled for twenty-four to thirty-six hours, absorbs the liquid and plumps." *Wow!* And that's just the pork chop. The service, architecture, and ambiance of this restaurant are definitive Sacramento at its best.

926 J St., 916-492-4450
grangerestaurantandbar.com

IMAX
THEATRE
ESQUIRE
IMAX
THEATRE
IMAX
THEATRE
NOW PLAYING
ASTEROID HUNTERS
SPIRAL

MUSIC AND ENTERTAINMENT

28

LIVE THE MOVIE

IMAX Corporation will tell you that any IMAX experience is a great experience. However, having been to the nation's top twenty-five IMAX locations, I can tell you that, with the exception of the Smithsonian Museum's IMAX, Sacramento's Esquire IMAX Theatre is the best immersion movie presentation you'll find. Originally a 1930s movie palace, and then many other things before returning to its theater glory, Esquire IMAX offers upscale food, beer, and wine. You'll recline comfortably in one of the 388 leather rocker seats while viewing IMAX's largest six-story-high, eighty-foot-wide screen, with eighteen thousand watts of digital wraparound sound. Prince, rest in peace, had this on his bucket list: in 2014 he rented the entire theater for a private date.

1211 K St., 916-443-4629
imax.com/imax-esquire-oo

DIE ON THE DELTA KING
BEFORE YOU DIE

Well, let's hope it's not you who gets offed at the Delta King Murder Mystery! This is a great night out for a multitude of reasons. It's located onboard a historic moored riverboat, and that's cool in itself. Your evening begins with a very nice dinner party in the original dining quarters of the ship. Then, without warning, someone gets whacked! You'll spend the rest of the evening trying to solve the murder mystery. This is great for a date or a group of up to 250! Highly recommended is the package in which you'll spend the night onboard in a stateroom and be treated to an amazing breakfast in the morning. The best bacon I've had in NorCal was on this boat. If someone had to die for great bacon, so be it!

1000 Front St., 916-444-5464
deltaking.com

SPOT THE COMEDY

Comedy Spot owner Brian Crall said, "I don't just want an improv club good enough for Sacramento, I want a club that would blow the doors off of any club in the world." And he accomplished that early on. You'll not find a funnier night of comedy than the prime-time, 9 p.m. Saturday night performance featuring his varsity troupe, the Anti-Cooperation League. The troupe has launched many a network career and routinely has drop-in guests from *Parks and Recreation* and *Kids in the Hall*, as well as Officer Byrd of *Judge Judy* fame. All shows here are good; ACL is exceptional.

1050 Twentieth St., #130, 916-444-3137
saccomedyspot.com

TIP

I'm also a huge fan of The Comedy Spot's Thursday night fun, Trash Movie Improv! That's a show in which a clip from a bad movie is played. After a few minutes the clip is suddenly stopped, and a team of improvisers must create new scenes based on the trash movie clip, all on the spot!

31

SPIKED FUN
IN THIS PUNCH BOWL

Imagine a twenty-five-thousand-foot playground wonderland of karaoke, bowling, virtual reality, billiards, other table games, darts, and vintage arcade machines. Add to that amazing food and craft cocktails. Throw in a private room for even more fun, and Punch Bowl Social is courtside to the Kings' Golden 1 Center. While playing around and chowing down you'll feel like a kid set loose in Bruce Wayne's library! Just bring yourself or your group, and they'll take care of the rest.

500 J St., Ste. 100, 916-925-5610
punchbowlsocial.com/location/sacramento

TIP

If you really want to go big, this place is within the complex of the Sawyer Hotel. Get a room!

32

ACE A CONCERT

Ace of Spades, although relatively new on the Sacramento live music scene, is a great place to see an act that would usually sell out a much larger venue. There are four bars, although most often the shows are all-ages, and there is a family-friendly area with great food. Warning—plan for a late night, as the acts don't always hit the stage on time. Once I was there to enjoy a Snoop Dogg show that was scheduled to start at 7:30 p.m.; he didn't take the stage until eleven. Wait . . . that was probably Snoop Dogg just being Snoop Dogg. Either way, check the schedule often for a diverse and impressive list of indie rock, pop, and hip-hop artists.

1417 R St., 916-930-0220
aceofspadessac.com

TIP

Best after-concert tacos ever—out the front door and across the street is Mas Taco Bar!

SACRAMENTO HAS SEVERAL TRIED-AND-TRUE LIVE MUSIC VENUES. ALSO CHECK OUT:

Old Ironsides

Old Ironsides has been jammin' since 1934. In fact, it received Sacramento's very first liquor license when Prohibition ended (although rumor has it that Prohibition didn't exactly slow their roll). Since that time, Old Ironsides has been offering up great music at a great price, anywhere from free to five dollars, plus food and beverage specials to match. Many Sacramento-turned-famous bands have rolled through here, including Cake and Papa Roach.

1901 Tenth St., 916-443-9751
theoldironsides.com

Harlow's Restaurant & Nightclub

This is as close to an old-fashioned supper club as you're going to get. Harlow's has a great dinner show, often followed by two later shows, featuring the best in blues, jazz, rock, and pop. Since 1982, this is where true music lovers have gone, and where musicians go to hear live music. Harlow's itself gets national acts, but don't be surprised to see the likes of Bruno Mars, after a sold-out arena show, chilling here to a live performance from the likes of one-time Prince protégé Andy Allo (yes, it happened).

2708 J St., 916-441-4693
harlows.com

33

EXPERIENCE BROADWAY

WAAAY OFF BROADWAY

When I first moved to Northern California, I was led by the hand to an out-of-place full-sized circus tent on a hot summer day, oddly located in the middle of downtown. Once inside the Music Circus I witnessed the best performance of *Cabaret* I've ever seen—and lost thirty pounds in water weight from all the sweat; it was one hundred degrees, and it's hard to air-condition a circus tent. The good news is that by the twenty-first century the tent was replaced by a permanent air-conditioned structure that is still tent-like on the inside! Now known as Broadway Sacramento, Sacramento's oldest professional performing arts company continues to entertain more than 250,000 patrons every year.

1510 J St., 916-446-5880
broadwaysacramento.com

34

BE
A COMEDY TEST AUDIENCE

Because Sacramento is such a demographic melting pot, it's often used by major corporations to test-market products to evaluate their effectiveness for the rest of America. Did you know the same is true for comedy? The secret's out! For decades comics have been sneaking into Sacramento to test their jokes on the eve of a *Tonight Show*, *Kimmel*, or *Conan* appearance to see if they're going to work on the national telecast. Two clubs offer exclusive stand-up. The more historic of the two is Laughs Unlimited, where Jerry Seinfeld worked out his act over twenty-seven appearances. Jay Leno and the late Garry Shandling and Robin Williams were also regulars when they were climbing the stand-up ranks. It was the unofficial bullpen for the Carson-era *Tonight Show* and still attracts national acts to its historic Old Sac room. The modern mecca of late-night comedy is Punch Line, located in a most unlikely strip mall, upstairs next to a mattress store. Dave Chappelle, Louis C. K., Mike E. Winfield, Amy Schumer, and a long list of others have made and continue to make the journey up the steps, past the Serta Perfect Sleeper, and onto the stage.

Laughs Unlimited, 1207 Front St., 916-446-8128
laughsunlimited.com

Punch Line, 2100 Arden Way, 916-925-8500
punchlinesac.com

DON'T
BE A SCROOGE

Any traces of your inner Scrooge will disappear if you go see the Theatre of Lights on Front and K streets. Words can't describe how magical, how world-class this event truly is. Each year, kicking off Thanksgiving Eve and running through Christmas Eve, this performance combining live action, digital projection, and multimedia art transforms a city block into a winter wonderland stage. Mark Twain steps out onto a balcony (the real balcony of the *Union* newspaper, where back in the day the real Mark Twain used to work) and assists in telling the story of *The Night Before Christmas.* Live appearances from pretty much everyone in that story, each night featuring a different local celebrity, are combined with digital mapping and special effects created exclusively by Skywalker Sound. If the narrator's voice sounds familiar, that's because it is Bill Farmer, the voice of Disney's Goofy.

K St. at Front St., Old Sacramento, 916-970-5226
godowntownsac.com

TIPS

Two shows run each night, usually but not always at 6:00 and 7:30 (check schedule). As with a Disney Main Street Parade, curbside is valued real estate, so get there early. There's great holiday shopping for unique small gifts at Stage Nine and Evangeline's (and great places to warm up). The best spot to watch is right in the middle of the street at 102 K Street (you'll see all the surprises on both sides, and because the big finish is the lighting of the official sixty-foot-tall tree, you'll have the best view of both the show and the tree! Light rail is a great way to avoid having to park, but if you must, best bets are Old Sacramento Garage (I and Second streets), Tower Garage (Capitol and Neasham), and Macy's West Garage (Third and L streets).

36

B IN A PLAY

The B Street Theatre is one of the nation's most respected professional theaters, started by award-winning television, film, and stage star Timothy Busfield and his equally talented brother Buck. Originally located on B Street (see, that's how it got its name!), it's now in the beautiful, new, state-of-the-art Sofia Tsakopoulos Center for the Arts (more simply known as "The Sofia") on Capitol Avenue at Twenty-Seventh Street. Since 1991, B Street Theatre is where audiences have turned to see the most popular and talked about plays of our day, and the new digs keep true to the intimate experience regular patrons have enjoyed over the years. Whether it's a mainstage production or the family series, seeing a play here will not likely be a once-in-a-lifetime experience—you'll hunger for more, and you will be back!

2700 Capitol Ave., 916-443-5300
bstreettheatre.org

ROCK
THE PARK

For more than twenty-five years, Sacramento has enjoyed the best free live music happy hour the state has to offer. Concerts in the Park happens every Friday at Cesar Chavez Plaza from 5 to 9 p.m., featuring multiple live bands. Some you've heard of (such as Cake, Tesla, and Deftones), some not so much, but they're all good! Food and beverages will cost you less than most festivals, and again, the concerts are *free* for all ages! Some of Sacramento's best local DJs will be spinning between sets. Nearby garages take care of your car, or arrive via RT light rail (try using the online trip planner at SacRT.com). There are even free bike valet services offered by SABA (Sacramento Area Bicycle Advocates). Concerts take place on Fridays during May, June, and July.

Cesar Chavez Plaza, 910 I St., 916-442-8575
godowntownsac.com

TESLA AND TACOS

Although Sacramento's famous metal band, Tesla, did play at Swabbies on the River, these days you're more likely to find a Jimmy Buffett, Gwen Stefani, Lynyrd Skynyrd, Steely Dan, Van Halen, or AC/DC cover band, plus a great view of the Sacramento River as it lazily rolls by and bawdy pirates greet you. Ahoy! You'll find tropic attitude aplenty! Grab something cold to drink, like one of the 19 beers they have on tap. Pair it with a signature Swabbies brisket taco, and enjoy the perfect outdoor concert picnic. If you're looking to get local, feel local, and seek a delta breeze on one of the famous 100 degree days we have in the valley, this is the spot! Beautiful sixty-foot trees will shade you, but if it looks like rain, call ahead.

5871 Garden Hwy., 916-920-8088
swabbies.com

CPR YOUR GROOVE
WITH REVIVAL

Revival bar and lounge's privileged rooftop location perched on the Sawyer Hotel puts you just a few steps away from Golden 1 Center, the home of the Sacramento Kings and music icon concerts. Revival's stylish indoor-outdoor lounge is the perfect place for a pre-game bite or a post-concert nightcap. Their lush seating amid wood and brass fixtures is also an amazing place to listen to DJ music alongside a sea of humanity dressed in impressive upscale cocktail attire, all moving in unison. Revival has the feel of Miami and/or Hollywood's Skybar.

500 J St., 916-399-4737
revivalsacramento.com

TIP

I highly recommend booking a room at the Sawyer Hotel. That gives you more exclusive access to Revival, which is hard to get in to on busy nights unless you're a guest. Plus, if your head is pounding from a big night, you'll thank me in the morning for being able to sleep in on the spot!

DANCE,
IN THE POOL

For nightlife, Faces historically has the best music, fifteen bars, three dance floors (one is Sacramento's biggest), and an open heated pool that anyone can use year-round. It's loud, wild, and best enjoyed in groups. And—oh yeah—it's also Sacramento's oldest and most populated gay club. Perhaps I should have led with that. I found out after the fact myself. I thought it was just a fitness club night out before I realized it was "out" out. Regardless, you'll find people of every orientation, no judging, and a good time here. And leave your cellphone at home just in case you have an unplanned pool dance.

2000 K St., 916-448-7798
faces.net

TIP

Be aware—if you're looking for an exclusively LGBTQ experience, this isn't the place. The crowd here has evolved to include all kinds of people. It is great if you are with a mixed group, and you will be guaranteed a welcoming rainbow of people once you're in with the "out."

FIND
ACOUSTIC SANCTUARY

On weekend nights the corner of Second and J streets in the old Sacramento Historic District belongs to Winko. This performance artist, a one-man band named Winko Ljizz, has a piano bar like no other. The Acoustic Sanctuary has four wheels, five stools, a one-couple dance floor, and a baby grand piano that seems to have been built into the van. Winko also has within his reach at all times dozens of musical instruments that he uses in sets consisting of "the hits of today and yesteryear." See this, but good luck trying to describe it to anyone! Winko sometimes changes locations, so be sure to check the website before you go.

200 J St., 916-454-9463
acousticsanctuary.com

TIP

Not so much a tip, but more of an understanding: because of this unique quirky one-person performing experience, you never know what you're going to get. Just as no two sunsets look the same, no two visits to see Winko are the same. Some days he's chatty, other days he's into more music and "back-to-back hits!"

42

SURVIVE
THE ROCKIN' RODEO

You'll survive, but you'll be sore after a night at Stoney's Rockin' Rodeo. I'm a city slicker, yet I feel transformed every time I leave this place. The staff and patrons are super-friendly, and it's infinitely more diverse than you'd expect. You will learn to line dance—*oh yes, you will*—it's not so much mandatory as it is infectious. Cheap drinks, good food, and horrible parking: trust me, you should Uber or Lyft in and out of this place for a multitude of reasons!

Country or not, you will spend most of your time dancing. And the dancing or the mechanical bull will leave your muscles remembering the great time you had for days!

1320 Del Paso Blvd., 916-927-6023
stoneyinn.com

VIP KARAOKE

Oishii Sushi and Heartbeat Karaoke might be the most upscale karaoke experience you've ever had, taking it to a whole new level. You get a private room (rooms for up to forty are available) and your own karaoke system. Each room is super-comfortable with wraparound furniture, as though it was designed by a limousine company. Bar and food service is controlled via an electronic pad in each room, as is the extensive big-screen, big-sound karaoke! The sushi is above average, and the experience is very special-occasion-worthy.

1000 K St., Ste. 200, 916-557-8088
oishiisushikaraoke.com

TIP

Warning—you need to know that this is a special occasion "big client out" sort of venue, and the prices reflect it. If you're on a budget, or just want to sample it, they do have happy hour reduced prices on food, beverage and spaces!

44

DON'T WAIT TO DRIVE IN

TO THE MOVIES

Sacramento is home to one of America's few remaining drive-in movie theaters, so before you die, see a movie on a drive-in screen before it dies! This is an unforgettable experience and a tribute to America's past. Family-owned and -operated since 1952, West Wind combines the old-school drive-in vibe with the latest technology, boasting the largest digital projectors available. And the audio is beamed straight to your car stereo! Pack your favorite tailgating supplies, get there before sunset, and toss a Frisbee or football around before the show. An extensive snack bar is at the center, and the show is always a double feature of first-run films! Re-enact the drive-in scenes from *Grease* or *Pee-wee's Big Adventure* while you wait. Please tweet and tag me if you actually do.

9616 Oates Dr., 916-363-6572
westwinddi.com

TIPS

If you've been to a drive-in movie these tips may seem ridiculously obvious. But for newcomers, here are items to make your outdoor movie-going experience a great one!

1. Don't try to sneak people in. They could die of carbon monoxide poisoning in your trunk, or you could die of embarrassment when you're caught and turned around to exit.

2. On a Friday or Saturday night they will sell out. Beat the rush by getting there at least an hour before sunset. To pass the time, bring dinner, drinks (no alcohol permitted) and maybe even a frisbee or ball to toss around to make the time fly!

3. Bring lawn chairs and blankets, and maybe even an outdoor radio or speaker; the sound for the movie plays through the FM radio in your car.

4. While SUVs backed in with the hatch up are the best way to lay out and be comfortable, you may be directed to the back rows as to not block the lower profile vehicles.

SPORTS AND RECREATION

SAY THAT YOU'VE BEEN
TO THE BEST BASKETBALL ARENA IN NORTH AMERICA

Taking in a Kings game or any event in Golden 1 Center will indeed be memorable. Inaugurated by rock royalty Sir Paul McCartney, G1 Center is "The Coliseum of the Twenty-First Century," with state-of-the-art technology in every aspect. G1 has the largest 4K indoor video screen in North America, roughly the size of the basketball court itself. HD screens are located at every possible angle so you don't miss a moment from anywhere. The G1 app will let you order food and beverage right to your seat. This is the most connected arena in the world, with more than one thousand access points to the fastest-streaming net in existence; it can handle five hundred thousand Snapchat posts per second! Acoustics were designed by the same group that upgraded Royal Albert Hall. You'll have no trouble remembering your experience because it's likely on your Snapchat Story!

500 David J Stern Walk, 888-91-KINGS (888-915-4647)
golden1center.com

46

WATCH RIVER CATS
IN THEIR NATURAL HABITAT

That is, see Sacramento's minor league baseball team, the Sacramento River Cats, play major-league-level ball in the beautiful $47 million stadium they call home. Baseball is America, and Sutter Health Field showcases the sport at its finest. The park, although in West Sacramento, offers you the best view of Sacramento, and there's not a bad seat in the venue. For less than half of what you would pay for parking at a Giants game, you can see the minor league team and the same major-league quality of play. Save even more by sitting in the grassy wraparound area beyond the outfield and you'll feel like you're part of the game!

400 Ballpark Dr., West Sacramento, 916-371-4487
sacramentorivercats.com

SEE A GOAAAAAAAAAAAAAAAAAAAAAL LIVE

Since 2014 Sacramento has been the proud home of the Republic FC professional soccer team. I'm honored to have been the inaugural announcer for the team's first game at Hughes Stadium, with a record crowd of more than twenty thousand fans. Since then their fan base has proliferated, and if you've never seen a pro soccer game, Republic FC home games are the perfect place to begin, as you'll witness world-class play and energy. There's not a bad seat at Papa Murphy's Park, home field for Republic FC. Some tips: get there early to get good seats, and take a pad or blanket if you're in general seating; those seats are best described as "the biggest rack of high school bleachers you've ever seen." And with that, depending on the season, your seat may be a tad chilly or warm.

1600 Exposition Blvd., 916-307-6100
sacrepublicfc.com

BE
THE PINBALL WIZARD

You don't have to be old enough to get that musical reference, or even to know what pinball is, to enjoy one of the most unique lounges of any city—the Coin-Op Game Room. You just have to be twenty-one or older to enjoy, and you *will* enjoy! In fact, I dare you not to have a good time there, surrounded by wall-to-wall classic video arcade games representing literally every era of gaming since Pong, along with the aforementioned grandfather to the video game—pinball. Great food, great mixologist cocktails, and even an outdoor patio, where giant Jenga and giant Connect Four games await your challenge. I travel all over the world for a living; not once have I seen the likes of this club. A must!

908 K St., 916-661-6983
coinopsac.com

49

LEARN TO BE
A PRO WAKEBOARDER WITHOUT A BOAT

Wake Island Waterpark is one of three cable-run wake parks in all of North America, and it is quite amazing. It is, without exaggeration, an oasis. On one side of the park is a continuous pull system for wakeboard towing. A handle is given to you as you stand on a dock, and the cable latches and pulls you around a perfect manmade lake, complete with optional jumps, kicks, and rails. And if you're more into watching than doing, do grab a beverage from the snack bar and sit on the ample sandy beach. On the other side of Wake Island is another mammoth manmade lake, this one filled corner to corner with a custom-made *Wipeout* TV show-style obstacle course. It's fun, but more challenging than you think. You will be getting wet and loving it. The sessions on the course last only thirty minutes, but I challenge you to last even that long!

7633 Locust Rd., Pleasant Grove, 916-655-3900
wakeislandwaterpark.com

50

REALLY SOAR
OVER CALIFORNIA

If you've ever been to Disney California Adventure Park to ride Soarin' Over California, the virtual flying experience, then imagine doing that in reality! Blue Sky PPG is one of the most unique, exciting, glorious experiences you'll find in this book. A powered-paragliding-certified instructor flies tandem with you over orchards and vineyards and along rivers and valleys in a fifteen- to forty-five-minute flight of a lifetime. It's not physically demanding, as the pilot does all the work. Powered paragliding is statistically one of the safest forms of sport aviation, and Blue Sky PPG is one of the best in the world. It is indeed a bucket-list-worthy experience. Takeoff and landing are less than thirty minutes from downtown Sacramento, but be sure to call ahead for an appointment.

1364 Sky Harbor Dr., Olivehurst, 530-308-3523
blueskyppg.com

LIVE THE *JUMANJI* LIFE
FOR REAL

Want to get up close and personal with an African spur-thighed tortoise? Ever wondered what it is like to hand-feed an okapi? Do you even have any idea what those things are? You can find out at the Sacramento Zoo via behind-the-scenes guided walking tours! You'll get one step closer than anyone else to amazing animals with these visits to areas that are not open to the general public. You'll feel like you're roaming the savanna and forests of Africa! Other tours include Hooves And Horns, and even alligators. Check ahead to see which tours are seasonally available.

3930 West Land Park Dr., 916-808-5888
saczoo.org

TIP

Build in time for a nice picnic after a long day of animal gazing, because conveniently located right across the street is one of California's largest and lushest most beautifully maintained parks!

52

THROW AN AXE
WHILE DRINKING BEER

Imagine mixing the throwing of sharp objects with alcohol . . . what could possibly go wrong? Check out the Smart Axe, one of America's premier axe-throwing pubs. It's about the biggest you'll find on the West Coast, with more than twenty-two lanes of WATL! What is WATL, you axe, I mean ask? It stands for the World Axe Throwing League. Throw in some of the region's finest microbrews on tap, and pow! That's entertainment! I swear, this is the best place in this entire book! (Disclaimer: Your humble author is a co-founder of this place.)

11151 Trade Center Dr., Rancho Cordova, 916-389-0178
thesmartaxe.com

TIP

Many people have described this as "darts on steroids," and upon trying, are instantly addicted. If you predict that this may happen to you, sign up at any location for league nights. There is indeed a world axe throwing league, and this establishment is certified WATL.

53

DANGLE PERILOUSLY UPSIDE DOWN

WHILE CLIMBING AN ARCH

Yes, you can do that, although you won't really be in much peril. At Sacramento Pipeworks, you'll find more than forty thousand square feet of climbing terrain and the largest indoor bouldering area on the West Coast. This is a great place for a date, as you'll need a climbing buddy to belay for you when you climb, and you do the same for him or her. What does that mean? Essentially, you'll climb in a harness attached to a safety rope, and the other end of that rope is harnessed to your buddy, who carefully tightens or loosens the rope as needed. It's much less complicated and much more fun than it sounds. If you've never climbed before, take the one-hour class and learn the basic skills needed to start. Back to that bouldering area: that's climbing without a rope; it's equally fun and safe, though a bit more challenging!

116 N Sixteenth St., 916-341-0100
touchstoneclimbing.com/pipeworks

SUP SAC

Sacramento has not one but two lovely flowing rivers, and undoubtedly one of the best ways to enjoy them is SUPing: stand-up paddleboarding. If you've never tried it, now is your chance! It takes a moment to learn, but thanks to this well-run company, Flow Stand Up Paddle, visitors and locals can rent equipment and get instruction on paddleboarding. The company also teaches SUP yoga and fitness and SUP race technique and even organizes SUP destination tours. It's a great way to spend an hour or a day, and it gives you some of the best views of the skyline as well as up-close encounters with indigenous creatures.

1501 Northgate Blvd., 916-599-6951
flowstanduppaddle.com

TIP

I would be negligent if I didn't mention that more drownings per capita happen at the convergence of the Sacramento and American rivers than in any other California waterway. So, always wear appropriate floatation devices out there, and be sure to tether your board. I don't want this to unexpectedly be the last thing on your "list."

HIT GOLF BALLS
OFF A ROOFTOP

Well, not exactly, though sort of . . . only better. It's hard to describe Topgolf except to say, imagine being in a one-block-long, three-story restaurant, with the entire back wall ripped off, then being invited to compete by hitting balls out of that open space to targets in the lot below. Now imagine that your ball has a micro-sensor in it, so scores for you and your family and friends can be tracked on the hundreds of giant LCD panels around you. Did I mention that it's hard to describe? This venue is amazing; it's about twenty-three minutes from downtown Sacramento but worth the drive. The food, beverages, and service are great, and the actual aforementioned point-scoring golf-like game is addictive. It's good for pro golfers, non-golfers, and five-to-105-year-olds alike. Be warned, this venue's sister property in Texas reports that people have moved nearby because of their passion for the product. Do this, and you may throw your other to-do-before-it's-all-over lists out the window. But not the window of this place; only golf balls are permitted to exit.

1700 Freedom Way, Roseville, 916-200-1002
topgolf.com/us/roseville

RUN
TO FEED THE HUNGRY

Having watched Run to Feed the Hungry grow from just around five hundred to more than twenty-five thousand people annually, this event is nearest and dearest to my heart. This Sacramento tradition since '94 is the largest Thanksgiving Day run in the country and directly benefits the Sacramento Food Bank. Join elite athletes from all over the world, as well as non-elite family and friends, all coming together for a great cause and a little calorie-burning before a lot of calorie consumption. The race weaves in and out of friendly neighborhoods. If it's your first time, it likely won't be your last.

J St., just West of the entrance to the Sacramento State campus, 916-456-1980
runtofeedthehungry.com

TIP

Plan on parking somewhere near the intersection of Howe Avenue and Fair Oaks Boulevard. That will add an extra half mile each way to your calorie burning endeavors! Did I see you wince at that? Then just Uber of Lyft it from there.

TRY NOT TO
SPOOK YOUR PANTS

Imagine being strapped to a flatbed truck, shooting paintballs at zombies while hurtling through a cornfield at breakneck speed! That's the Zombie Attack, and it's just one of the scary things you'll experience as Corbett's House of Horror presents Fear Farm. Trust me, this ain't your father's haunted house. Try to *not* get lost in the Scarecrow Corntrail four-acre haunted corn maze. Other fully haunted attractions include the Carn-Evil and Medical Mayhem. Come for set design, fog and lighting, live actors, and incredible effects you've never seen before, constructed by nationally recognized set designers. If you live for Halloween fun, Corbett's Fear Farm is the place to be. Open weekends and Halloween in October.

46500 County Rd. 32B, Davis, 916-303-7786
corbettshouseofhorror.com

TIP
Scare easily? You might want to bring a change of underwear.

SKYDIVE
INDOORS

Why take the risk of jumping out of a perfectly good airplane when you can strap on a wing suit and jump into a wind tunnel to experience the same thrill? At iFLY Indoor Skydiving, training and flying take about an hour and a half, and the actual flight is longer than the flight time of real skydiving. You'll get flight training; they'll gear you up with a helmet, flight suit, and goggles; and after the flight you'll get a commemorative personalized flight certificate to show your friends. Want a video of your flight? That's available too. It's good for ages three to 103, but you need to be reasonably fit and healthy to participate; there are some weight and health restrictions, so check the website first. Then have a nice float!

118 Harding Blvd., Roseville, 916-836-4359
iflyworld.com/sacramento

SAIL AWAY

Learn to sail in only a day (or two)! The Sacramento State Aquatic Center is a great place to begin your pursuit of sailing. The two-day course will get you certified to rent boats on this gorgeous part of the American River known as Lake Natoma and will get you prepped for experiences on bigger boats and bigger bodies of water. Just want to get on the water for a floating picnic or leisurely paddle? The center offers rentals of just about every personal watercraft you would want. Training takes place about fifteen miles east of the actual Sac State campus.

1901 Hazel Ave., Gold River, 916-278-2842
sacstateaquaticcenter.com

TIP

Planning to stay for the day? Just adjacent to the Aquatic Center you'll find great picnicking areas and some nice sandy beaches.

60

GET READY
FOR THE BOSTON MARATHON

. . . by starting with the California International Marathon! What began humbly in 1983 has become a world-class running event. It's a very fast point-to-point marathon, with a spectacular finish in front of the California State Capitol. It is certified and sanctioned by USATF and is a qualifier for both the Boston Marathon and the Olympic Marathon Trials. The race takes place in December, but entries are usually filled up by September. The California International Marathon is for the able, ready, and trained and is to be taken quite seriously. For the rest of us, feel free to goof around on the 2.62-mile maraFUNrun and Fitness Walk that happen concurrently.

916-737-2627
runcim.org

61

DANGLE OVER THE DELTA
ON A KITEBOARD

You may have seen thrill seekers zooming, jumping, and shredding on a wakeboard, apparently strapped by harness to a big kite. And you may have said, "I'd never do that." Well, never say never, because now you have reason to do so. Most locals don't even realize that for sixty to ninety days out of the year, the Sacramento area has the two key ingredients that make it a kiteboarding mecca: perfectly constant fifteen-to-twenty-five-knot winds and an open body of water. Kiteboarders from all points of the globe often relocate here during this time, via toy haulers, campers, tents, or whatever in order to harness the perfect breeze. If you're ready to try it, Nat Lincoln, a former world champion who lives in Hawaii and Mexico during perfect wind portions of the year, will teach you how to do it, from absolute beginner to being able to buy your own gear and enjoy the sport safely. His company, Edge Kiteboarding, opens and closes on Sherman Island each season with the wind, and you'll be able to track the dates online.

West Sherman Island Rd. on Sherman Island, Rio Vista, 775-721-1132
edgekiteboarding.com

SWIM
LIKE A GOLD MEDALIST

Book a room and buy a day pass, or if you're the country club type, buy a membership to Arden Hills Athletic & Social Club. Since it opened in 1954, athletes who have trained at Arden Hills have collectively set more than two hundred world and American records and earned thirty-one Olympic medals, including twenty-one gold, seven of which were won by legendary swimmer Mark Spitz. Mark Spitz swam in this pool, and you can too, if you have the means to do so (said in my finest Ferris Bueller tone). It is quite lovely, and I don't say "lovely" very often.

1220 Arden Hills Ln., 916-482-6111
ardenhills.club

TIP

Planning some nuptials? They have excellent event facilities, and are actually one of Sacramento's top three destinations for weddings!

63

LIVE A FAIRYTALE LIFESTYLE FOR FREE

Sacramento has a park with giant artifacts from all the children's classic fairy tales. You know the old woman who lived in a shoe? You'll find her house-sized shoe here. Humpty Dumpty's bridge? That's here too, and a lot more, with plenty of attractions, animals, gardens, and stages. The park is open year-round, but once a year, on December 24, you can get into Fairytale Town for free. With the park decorated for the holidays, it's a wonderful way to spend Christmas Eve day, kids or no kids. If kids are a part of the plan, it's a great way to burn off the energy they have built up in excitement and anticipation for the big day.

3901 Land Park Dr., 916-808-5233
fairytaletown.org

64

JUMP OUT
OF A PERFECTLY GOOD AIRPLANE

Okay, so this has been on the bucket list of just about everyone since the sport of skydiving was invented. The Sacramento area is home to the Parachute Center, a world-class training center, and in fact it is one of the oldest and largest drop zones in the nation. Did you see the squirrel suit stunt sequences in *Transformers* or *Point Break*? They trained for that here. So maybe you're not ready for that, but you'd like to jump out of a perfectly good airplane while strapped to someone who knows what they're doing? This is the place. It comes with risks, but so did the twenty-three-mile drive to get here, and you didn't sign a waiver for that, did you?

23597 N Hwy. 99, Acampo, 209-369-1128
parachutecenter.com

65

HEAR SOMEONE SAY
"IF IT AIN'T RUBBIN' IT AIN'T RACIN'" IN CONTEXT

That is to say, see, hear, and feel the fury of a real NASCAR race live! The All American Speedway is a NASCAR-sanctioned track, and though the track is open year-round, make it your goal to see the ARCA Menards Series West (formerly known as the NASCAR K&N Pro Series West) every October at this track. It's a relatively small oval, and there's not a bad seat in the stands. And don't be surprised if you end up rubbing elbows with a genuine NASCAR star or two watching alongside you. Many up-and-comers and at-the-top-of-their-game racers enjoy the track for scouting and evaluating other drivers! I once saw Hailie Deegan in the stands. She's the first woman to win the NASCAR WEST series. If you're a fan, you likely already knew that! Twenty-two minutes from downtown. Git 'er dun! (Start practicing your NASCAR-speak on the drive up.)

800 All America City Blvd., Roseville, 916-786-2025
allamericanspeedway.com

66

EXPERIENCE
THE ROARING THRILL OF CLASS 2 RAFTING RAPIDS

If you know anything about rafting, you know that "Class 2" isn't exactly roaring; in fact it's barely a ripple. But that's only ten seconds out of your three-and-a-half-hour lazy float down the American River. Most of it is self-guided, so you can just sit there and relax in your raft on your Class 1 journey. Though not challenging, it is a fun, potentially relaxing, potentially wild day—depending on how you do it. You can rent rafts for two to twelve people and even join several rafts together to form your own floating festival. Simply let the current take you while you picnic, organize water cannon shootouts, have races, or invent your own river ritual. American River Raft Rentals has been doing it the longest and will help you make the most of your day. Expect to carry a big, sturdy raft about one-quarter mile down a road, through a trail, and into the river. Fortunately, about three and a half hours later (in my experience, right when you're ready to get out), you're at the correct time and place to get out, and you simply beach the raft and the company's crew does the rest. Then you'll wait a few minutes for a shuttle that takes you back to where you parked your car.

11257 S Bridge St., Rancho Cordova, 888-338-7238
raftrentals.com

TIPS

- To make it super-relaxing, get more raft than you need: Two people? Get a four-person raft. Six? Get the twelve.
- Wear sunscreen!
- Double zip-lock anything that shouldn't get wet, especially cellphones!
- Triple-secure your car keys because many get lost on the journey.
- Better to take more small ice chests than one big one.
- Take ample snacks, food, and beverages, but know that alcohol is banned on holiday weekends.
- On super-hot days, a sunbrella will be your friend!

BIKE
THE AMERICAN RIVER TRAIL

You could easily make this an entire day, or just a great hour. I did the latter, and only decades later found out that this glorious paved bike, run, walk, skate, crawl (OK, you get it) trail is thirty-two miles long! It is actually known by two names: The American River Bike Trail, and the Jedediah Smith Memorial Trail. Following the edges of the American River as it flows through natural beauty, the area is protected and preserved by the American River Parkway Foundation. One end of the trail is at Discovery Park in Old Sacramento, and the other at Folsom Lake's southwestern banks at Beal's Point. The bike path bumps into the Sacramento Northern Bikeway just before Del Paso Boulevard near Railroad Drive. There are mile markers, trailside maps, water fountains, restrooms, and telephones all along this this two-lane trail, and many places to stop to for food, rest, or just to take in the breathtaking scenery. For the most part the American River Trail is shaded and level, though in some places you'll encounter some rolling hills. Travel far enough and you'll go through a few parks and swimming areas, and the suburban enclaves of Sacramento.

905 Leidesdorff St., Folsom, 916-706-0077
practicalcycle.com

NOTE

Don’t panic, but be aware: about two miles of the trail is on-road in a designated bike lane, and parts are shared by many different users, including equestrians. There are places to rent bikes at several points, including Practical Cycle Transportation Company. Just make sure you get geared up with a proper helmet, lock, and maybe a handlebar bag.

SEE FIREWORKS
ON THE HORNBLOWER

Old Sacramento has fantastic Fourth of July fireworks, and the greatest way to see them is in the middle of the Sacramento River, complete with city skyline, Tower Bridge, and the Delta King all in your sights. An Independence Day ticket is hard to get, but certainly worth the effort. Hornblower Riverboat excursions can also be booked for private parties, weddings, special events, or simply one-hour sightseeing year-round. For less than you think, you can pick a date (maybe your "special" date), choose your food, your music, and your own personalized route. If you play your cards right, maybe they'll actually let you toot the Hornblower's horn!

1206 Front St., 916-446-1185
hornblower.com/sacramento

69

TAKE
THE URBAN QUEST

One of the best, most unique ways to have fun in our great city and quickly fall in love with Sacramento is by playing Urban Adventure Quest, an app-based walking tour game. Grab some friends or family and divide into two teams (each with a fully charged smartphone), download the app, sign up, and get ready to go! I've never enjoyed Sacramento more, and in fact five items in this book came from discoveries on my Urban Adventure Quest. Each team is given simultaneous clues and cues to a walking tour of the city. It costs about fifty dollars per team, and each team can have up to five people. Your journey will take about two hours (not including any stops for food, beverage, or breaks). Do it!

Starts at Capitol Ave. and Sixteenth St. (the app will guide you)
805-603-5620, urbanadventurequest.com

70

JET SKI
FOLSOM LAKE

While there is nothing unique to jet skiing on a lake, within a very short time after experiencing a hundred-plus-degree day in Sacramento, you'll be one hundred percent into it! The hotter it gets, the more perfectly temperate Lake Folsom becomes. And there's no better way to have fun in our blue Northern California jewel than by borrowing someone else's jet ski. I've tried not to name-drop excessively on this list, but the one and only time I rented at Granite Bay Rentals, Eddie Murphy and his family (who at the time lived a mile away from this beach) were doing the same. Prices are about what you'd pay anywhere, at any resort, for hourly and day rentals.

Granite Bay boat launch at Folsom Lake, 916-910-5335
granitebaypwcrentals.com

71

DON'T SCREAM
ON THE SCREAMER

The story of this ride is almost, but not quite, as fun as the ride itself. It opened at Scandia in 2008, and within weeks, a city ordinance was passed making it illegal for anyone to scream on the Sky Screamer. It turns out that whisking people at fifty-five miles an hour 155 feet into the air and then hurtling them over the freeway and toward the ground (repeatedly) created a bit of a noise disturbance for local neighbors. Most people comply, and no scream arrests have been reported. Before or after you hold your screams, enjoy the mini-rollercoaster, mini-golf, batting cages, bumper boats, and hundreds of arcade options.

5070 Hillsdale Blvd., 916-331-5757
scandiafun.com

TIP

Parents, dropping the kids off for a couple of hours of fun? Your own entertainment is right down the street at Stones Gambling Hall casino. You'll find Vegas-level luxury card playing, great American-style food, and craft beers. And don't worry, I won't tell the kids where you've been.

72

SKATE OR DIE,
BEFORE YOU DIE

Take a skateboarding lesson or just come to watch some of the nation's best skateboarding at 28th & B St. Skate Park, an amazing city-run indoor skateboarding park. Omar Salazar, former world champion and one of the more famous skateboarders from Sacramento, inaugurated this ten-thousand-square-foot skateboard hangar. It costs three bucks to use the facility, but it's well worth it. Pad and helmet rentals are only one dollar. Skateboarders have long had reputations for being pirates on wheels, and not exactly open to outsiders. But that's not the case here, as I found them to be welcoming, helpful, and friendly. And I'm an old guy! Dude, do it!!

20 Twenty-Eighth St., 916-494-8724
cityofsacramento.org/28andB

TIP

Dawgpound Skateshop on Del Paso is my favorite place to buy boards and gear—if you're trying to be legit!

73

SEE
THE BUG RACES

Sacramento has a long tradition of motorsports. In fact, in his youth, George Lucas once raced a car at Sacramento Raceway Park. But nothing here is quite as unique as the biannual (spring and fall) Bugorama, the nation's largest and longest-running VW event. Thousands of people and hundreds of Volkswagen bugs from all over the world arrive to showcase, race, and worship the mighty Beetle. Though the bug is the star, you'll also see hundreds of the even more rare VW bus, the Karmon Ghia, and the VW Thing. Please act like you don't know, and ask an owner about one of the latter, "Hey, what's that thing?" They'll laugh and laugh and answer like it's the first time that they have heard that question.

5305 Excelsior Rd., 800-929-0077
bugorama.com

CULTURE AND HISTORY

SCHMOOZE
WITH POLITICIANS

Did you know that you can walk right in and visit your local representative (if you're a Californian) at the State Capitol? That is one of several reasons to visit! At the California State Capitol, the past, present, and future of California interact with equal force. The building serves as both a museum and the state's working seat of government. Visitors to the Capitol can experience California's rich history and witness the making of future history through the modern lawmaking process. It's a beautiful part of California history. Visit to wander, but if you're hoping to see your favorite policy wonk, know that post-pandemic, many of them may work from home, on the road, or in DC.

1315 Tenth St., 916-324-0333
capitolmuseum.ca.gov

TIPS

Visit the gift shop in the basement, and get your shoes shined at the lower south exit. You'll likely be getting the same shine that many a senator and three United States presidents received. Also, although it takes time, negotiation, and a screening process, there are limited tours of the actual dome itself—a truly once-in-a-lifetime experience.

75

GO OFF THE RAILS
IN A CRAZY TRAIN . . . MUSEUM

You might think you have an idea of what a train museum would be like, until you step into rail history at the California State Railroad Museum, spread across one hundred thousand square feet in six buildings. Until you've stood grill to grill with a 120-plus-ton locomotive, you have no real appreciation for the awesome industrial proportion and magnitude of these giant vehicles. You'll find several of those beasts, with just about every other kind of train in the history of rail transportation. There's a twenty-minute movie that gets you up to speed, and you'll meet some of the finest, most committed docents you'll ever find, dare I say, at any museum.

125 I St., 916-323-9280
csrmf.org

TIP

This may give away where my mind tends to linger . . . this is one of two donut tips for you. If you're famished after a day of Trainspotting, right out the front door of the Railroad Museum you walk into Danny's Mini Donuts. You're welcome.

ROLL
BY THE REAGANS

While technically there are three houses you could see if presidential residential visits are on your bucket list, I'll skip #1 and #3, and here's why: Ronald Reagan lived in the actual Governor's Mansion for only a few months before Nancy orchestrated a move. She decided that the mansion would make a better museum than home. Plus, the twelve-thousand-square-foot home they were constructing in Carmichael didn't get finished in time. So the Reagans found a house in Sacramento's famous and exclusive Fab 40s neighborhood. There you'll find the cozy six-thousand-square-foot, six-bedroom, four-bath place they called home. It's on a lovely tree-lined and ungated street, ready for your photo op. But take your picture from the street or sidewalk; don't trespass or you'll wish you had Secret Service protection!

1341 Forty-Fifth St.

77

PARTY
IN THE MOVIE PALACE

See, do, participate in anything at the Crest Theatre, a grand 1912 vaudeville theater-turned-movie palace! The Crest was converted to its current glorious form in the 1950s, and has remained untouched ever since. Take in a concert, comedian, or movie here, and your experience will be elevated by the impressive history and vibe of this venue. You may dine pre-show in the full-service Empress Tavern restaurant on site, named after this theater's historic original title. Or have a bite along the K Street walking neighborhood. In fact, many of the best eats in town are within a two minute stroll in any direction from here. Words can't describe the beauty of the restoration of this architectural work of art. A little word of warning: if you're a fan of the lay-back, super large, comfortable chairs that are now cinema standard, you won't find them here. Seating, like everything else here, leans original.

1013 K St., 916-476-3356
crestsacramento.com, empresstavern.com

78

KILLER PHOTO OP

I'm sorry for putting this in, but not all history is pretty. At this location, you'll find an unassuming boarding house, once run by Dorothea Puente, a sweet little thing who looked a bit like Granny, the owner of Tweety in the old *Looney Tunes* cartoons. However, she had a habit of renting rooms to the elderly, stealing their Social Security checks, killing anyone who complained, and burying them in the backyard. This "I would have gotten away with it if not for you meddling kids" villain became known as the "Death House Landlady" after she dispatched nine of her tenants and used them as fertilizer by the time of her arrest. Technically speaking, a couple of them were used as a foundation for a paved patio. London has its Jack the Ripper tours, and you can see Lizzie Borden's place in Boston. Here in Sacramento, visit Dorothea's. I've seen people stop, jump out of a car, snap a selfie in front of this house, and move on. Super creepy. Don't block the current owner and don't linger too long. Especially not at night (insert maniacal laugh here).

1426 F St.

79

SEIZE THE TOWER

The legendary vinyl emporium Tower Records, the ground zero of the chain that was where "rock stars bought records," no longer exists. Then Tower gave way to Dimple Records, a slightly younger record shop in the same building. Alas, Dimple is no more, and the tradition now rests with Phono Select Records, albeit in a different location. It is known as Sacramento's friendliest and coolest record store, and you'll find a most well-organized selection of new and used vinyl records, tapes, CDs, books, magazines, and even some toys and vintage clothing. All the cool kids shop there . . . join the vinyl re-revolution by picking up a classic disc or two.

2475 Fruitridge Rd., 916-400-3164
phonoselect.com

TIP

Need a turntable to play your records? Delta Breeze at 1715 10th Street has a smaller selection of vinyl than Phono Select, but a great selection of used players!

NOTE

For the historically curious, you may still see the original Tower sign, as it is preserved in the Golden 1 Center. And the theater named after the record palace and its iconic art-deco tower is across the street from the original location, at 2508 Land Park Drive. The movie written and directed by former Sacramentan Tom Hanks, *That Thing You Do!*, pays tribute to a small appliance store that ended up also selling records, and Tom's Sacramento-native son Colin Hanks directed the critically acclaimed documentary *All Things Must Pass: The Rise and Fall of Tower Records*.

80

DON'T TOUR
THE HISTORIC GOVERNOR'S MANSION

. . . because California's governor is likely in there right now! The Governor's Mansion housed California governors from 1903 to 1967 and became open to the public as Governor's Mansion State Historic Park by the 1970s. However, Governor Jerry Brown, who during his first two terms slept on a mattress in a small downtown apartment, decided to have the mansion renovated and restored as an official residence for himself and successive California governors. The mansion remains highly visible from the street, so at least stop by, take your pic, and say you were there. You won't see the $16,000 refrigerator that was part of the extreme kitchen makeover, nor will you see the 1902 Steinway piano that remains from the Pardee administration. But you will see a gorgeous three-story, thirty-room Second Empire-Italianate Victorian mansion that was built in 1887.

1526 H St.

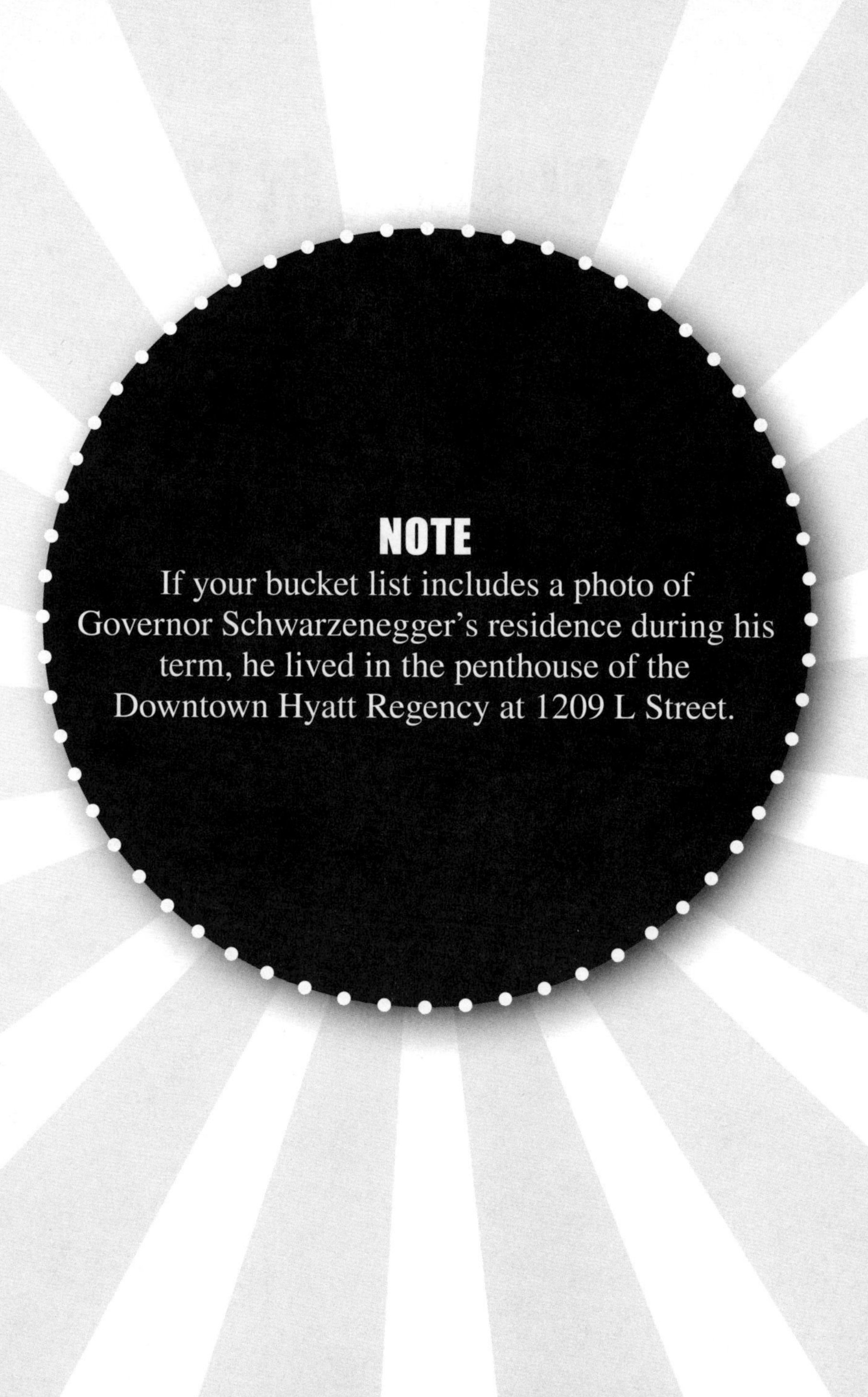

NOTE
If your bucket list includes a photo of Governor Schwarzenegger's residence during his term, he lived in the penthouse of the Downtown Hyatt Regency at 1209 L Street.

81

TRAVEL BACK IN TIME
IN A DELOREAN

Well, at least see an original, genuine (non-movie prop) DeLorean, as well as hundreds of other amazing automobiles in the billion-dollar collection at the California Automobile Museum. Speaking of a billion dollars, did you know that Malcolm Forbes had a money-green Lamborghini Countach given to him as a gift? He evidently didn't need it and regifted it to this museum. The first car donated to the museum, a 1938 Buick Sedan, is on display along with plenty of other cool cars, trucks, and even RVs. Give yourself plenty of time to stroll the more than seventeen thousand square feet of automotive history. This is one of Sacramento's hidden gems, but hopefully not that hidden anymore after this publication!

2200 Front St., 916-442-6802
calautomuseum.org

JOIN
THE GREAT ART DEBATE

Since 1967, Chicago has had a giant Afghan dog-meets-woman sculpture by Pablo Picasso on display, and to this day people stand around and debate whether it should or should not occupy valuable real estate in the Windy City. The same is true of Jeff Koons's *Coloring Book No. 4*, one of the most expensive art risks in Sacramento's history. This multi-million-dollar, eighteen-foot-tall hunk of cartoonish color and steel can be seen at the entrance of Golden 1 Center. Full disclosure: this author is friends with internationally recognized pop artist David Garibaldi, and I wanted his work here. Although I do love Koons's work, my thought is that *Coloring Book No. 4* would look lovely in Koons's hometown of York, Pennsylvania. But that's the beauty of art—everybody sees things differently. Now go take a look for yourself, and then discuss!

Golden 1 Center, on Fifth Street between J and L streets

AWAKEN
YOUR PIONEER SPIRIT AT SUTTER'S FORT

History buff or not, visit Sutter's Fort State Historic Park and you will walk away knowing that you were in the oldest restored fort in the United States! In 1839, Swiss immigrant John Sutter received a land grant from the Mexican government and built an agricultural empire, which he named New Helvetia (New Switzerland). Right in the heart of Midtown Sacramento, this place takes you back to the pioneer spirit of families arriving in wagon trains during the California Gold Rush, a pivotal time and place in California history. Some areas are fully restored, while restoration projects in other areas of Sutter's Fort are ongoing. Committed docents in character are on hand for this mostly self-guided tour, and there are year-round special programs and events.

2701 L St., 916-445-4422
suttersfort.org

PILOT
YOUR OWN ADVENTURE

Experience the awe and mystery of outer space and high-flying jets . . . with your feet firmly planted on the ground. The Aerospace Museum of California, on the grounds of the former McClellan Air Force Base, spans more than four acres, along with the thirty-five-thousand-square-foot Hardie Setzer Pavilion. You can get up close and personal with flying machines and apparatus, from vintage fully restored piston aircraft to modern jet and rocket engines. How about stepping right up to a US Navy Blue Angel fighter or a *Top Gun* F-15 Tomcat? Want to learn what it's like to be an actual pilot? You can with the Flight Zone flight simulator, a state-of-the-art STEM learning laboratory featuring ten digital flight stations, where you'll be trained by experienced volunteer flight instructors. Want to find out what a trip to Mars will look like in the year 2034? Set up a formal tour, or just zoom on in!

3200 Freedom Park Dr., McClellan, 916-643-3192
aerospaceca.org

85

SEE MILLIONS
OF MILLION-DOLLAR LIGHTS

While Sacramento and its suburbs have dozens of amazing cooperative efforts by homeowners to create dazzling streets of holiday lights, the original must-see is the Fabulous 40s neighborhood. Streets numbered in the 40s in the Sacramento area are a collection of beautifully restored and renovated million-dollar-plus mansions. Think “original Beverly Hills,” and replace the palms with oak trees. Each holiday season, residents in this area pay someone who pays someone to put up impressive displays. Some houses join together for extended displays; others light up individually, and they all crisscross the streets. It is majestic and not to be missed; see it at least once in your lifetime. Traffic gets heavy with cars, limos, and even party bikes and horse-drawn wagons! Be patient, and if you have time to see only a few, make it Forty-Second to Forty-Fifth streets.

Fortieth to Forty-Ninth streets,
between H Street and Folsom Boulevard

GET A CONTACT HIGH
IN MEMORIAL AUDITORIUM

Don't worry, you won't, but for a very long time the myth persisted that so much "residue" from late '60s-era concert crowds lingered in the ceiling of this classic venue that you might get altered yourself just by breathing there. Opened in 1927 and remodeled in 1997 (with a thorough scrub of that ceiling), Memorial Auditorium remains one of the most recognizable and beloved buildings in the region and is listed on the National Register of Historic Places. Big bands and violin virtuosos opened the place, and the Beach Boys and Rolling Stones recorded here. See a concert or comedian, or rent the place out for a wedding or special event. Dubbed "Sacramento's Carnegie" by me, just now . . . but a well-deserved title!

1515 J St., 916-808-5291
sacramentomemorialauditorium.com

GO UNDERGROUND

Sacramento founders got tired of having to repair and rebuild downtown every time the river overflowed, so they eventually built the town on top of the town, leaving the original largely intact in places below ground. Technically speaking, they "jacked up" much of the town in a process much more fun to see than to read about. Tour guides from the Sacramento History Museum will explain as you explore two spaces that were created by the city's successful raising process. This historical tour includes hollow sidewalks, sloped alleyways, and the underground spaces themselves. A colorful cast of guides ensures that no two tours are ever the same! Historical as well as specialty haunted tours are available.

101 I St., 916-808-7059
sachistorymuseum.org

GO TO CHURCH BEFORE YOU DIE

OR AFTER

I said that mostly to tie into the theme of the book, which is never a bad idea. Do see, both inside and out, the Cathedral of the Blessed Sacrament, considered to be both a religious and a civic landmark. It is the largest of its kind west of the Mississippi, and because of its size it has been used as the location for funeral services for former governors of California. Modeled after L'Église de la Sainte-Trinité (the Church of the Holy Trinity) in Paris, with a central bell tower rising 215 feet, this cathedral is a sight to behold. In fact, grab a table and have a cup of coffee across the street at Ambrosia Café for the best vista and street ambiance you'll have in this town. Though this is an active cathedral year-round, there is a gift shop, and tours can be booked on site.

1019 Eleventh St., 916-444-3071
cathedralsacramento.org

SPEND THE NIGHT,
PERHAPS YOUR LAST, IN THE PRESTON CASTLE

One look at the Preston Castle and you'll shudder at the possibility of actually entering, let alone the idea of spending the night inside with real ghostbusters. One of the oldest and best-known reform schools in the United States, it opened in 1894 housing wards of the state transferred from San Quentin State Prison. Stories of horror and haunting, both real and myth, abound; you'll hear more about them once inside (insert evil laugh here). Since it was vacated in 1960, little has been done to restore or de-creep the building, now an official California Historical Landmark listed on the National Register of Historic Places. The Preston Castle has been immortalized in the award-winning feature film *Apparition*, starring Mena Suvari (*American Horror Story*, *American Pie*) and Kevin Pollak (*Marvelous Mrs. Maisel*, *The Usual Suspects*). A must see before you die, and perhaps after (insert another evil laugh here). Overnight haunted tours are best, and even better if on a Friday the 13th or Halloween!

900 Palm Dr., Ione, 209-256-3623
prestoncastle.com

90

BE A PART OF THE SCANDAL, OR SEVERAL

The Citizen Hotel is worth a visit or stay for a multitude of reasons. Construction began on this high-rise at about the same time as New York's Empire State Building in the 1920s, and the building has some of the same architectural cues. However, the Citizen Hotel opened first and these days contains some of Sacramento's finest restaurants. Grange Restaurant & Bar here is always spectacular. Scandal is an informal bar area located in a loft right over the check-in desk. The motif is that of a law library, paying tribute to some of the early Sacramento law firms that began in this building. One entire wall is lined with autographs from famous guests who have signed a Scandal napkin. The fun here is to carefully look at the signatures and discover some famous people who in fact went on to have real-life scandals. I'm not revealing who they are here. Go see for yourself!

926 J St., 916-447-2700
thecitizenhotel.com

91

GET NAKED
IN PUBLIC AT LAGUNA DEL SOL

I was trying to think of a clever, punnier way of saying it, but I opted to just call it what it is. If spending time at a nudist resort is something you need to get out of the way, here it is! Don't judge me; I had to try it on for size during a (heavily pixelated) live broadcast not too long ago, and honestly the experience dispelled many of my preconceived ideas. As the Laguna del Sol clothing-optional resort says on its brochure, it has "members and guests of all ages, races, shapes, and sizes . . . a typical cross-section of the general public, with maybe just a little more willingness to try new and different experiences." We all spend a lot of time adjusting clothing; imagine not doing or having to think about that all day. Now that's freedom! You'll drive about twenty-five minutes out of downtown for this special brand of freedom. This full-service resort has everything you would expect from a country club, including pools, spas, a fitness center, a lake, and overnight accommodations . . . all clothing-optional. Here's a little tip: bring sunscreen, lots of sunscreen!

8683 Rawhide Ln., Wilton, 916-687-6550
lagunadelsol.com

GET YOURSELF ON LOCK
. . . IN LOCKE

Locke is a must-see stop on your Sacramento trip, located steps away from the Sacramento Delta. In 1971 Locke was added to the National Register of Historic Places by the Sacramento County Historical Society because of its unique status as the only town in the United States built exclusively by the Chinese for the Chinese. And what remains there today is truly remarkable and indescribable. It's not a tourist trap, and it's not a ghost town. Two blocks of the original settlement remain intact and unchanged. You'll find a boarding house museum and a gambling museum, both pointing to Locke's busy past. By the 1940s, restaurants, bakeries, herb shops, fish markets, gambling halls, boarding houses, brothels, grocery stores, a school, clothing stores, and the Star Theatre all lined the bustling streets. Visitors are welcome to Locke, and there are no fees for visiting. The entire town is a historical site, but is also a living community; therefore, respect the privacy of Locke's residents. And don't visit without stopping by Al's Place for lunch: you can't miss it, it's just about all that's open, and it's a remarkable family-run bar/restaurant that continues to get rave reviews from the masses. It's the best in town . . . yes, the only one in town, but still very good!

Locke Visitors Center, 13916 Main St., Locke, 916-776-1684
locke-foundation.org

93

WORK
ON YOUR WARHOL AT THE CROCKER ART MUSEUM

. . . while also hanging out in the longest continuously operating art museum in the West. The Crocker Art Museum hosts one of the state's premier collections of Californian art dating from the Gold Rush to the present day, a collection of master drawings, European paintings, and one of the largest international ceramics collections in the United States. It also hosts tours of the most celebrated artists in the world, such as Toulouse-Lautrec, Warhol, and others. Be sure to check the website or call ahead to find out which touring exhibitions are currently on site. The museum offers classes in art appreciation, hands-on painting, and ceramics as well. The facility itself is a world-class destination; the original mansion, built in the 19th century, is now joined to 135,000 square feet of modern architectural wonder!

216 O St., 916-808-7000
crockerartmuseum.org

DO GO
TO DOCO

Sacramento's Downtown Commons, known by the shortened name DOCO, is an entertainment and lifestyle outdoor plaza district, a few steps away from the State Capitol and Old Town Waterfront and right next to Golden 1 Center. Surrounded by great shopping, restaurants, theaters, and hotels, it's where locals like to hang out year-round, and visitors from around the globe experience the city at its finest. And every fall thousands flock to the annual DOCO Block Party. It's free, open to all ages, and filled with tons of entertainment, live music, hands-on art activities, displays, special activities in the shops, and plain old outdoor fun! And did I mention that it's free? Oh—for the inaugural event in 2019, live music included pop icon Vanilla Ice, who, um, iced it, baby! Check the website to find out exactly when this year's boffo DOCO happens.

SHOPPING AND FASHION

BE THE MASTER
OF YOUR OWN DISGUISE DOMAIN AT EVANGELINE'S

Evangeline's is one of the best novelty gift shops you will ever set foot in anywhere, and it's also one of the nation's biggest year-round costume shops. You really need to go here to see true Sacramento history. Not many places can say they were once a brothel and at a later time a disco, in two different centuries. Evangeline's is in one of only four buildings to have survived the fire that destroyed much of downtown in 1852. It also survived its discotheque years to become what it is today. There is something absolutely silly for everyone among the endless aisles of "stuff" downstairs and two floors of the Costume Mansion above. Take the fully restored turn-of-the-twentieth-century elevator to the upper floors! Very Tower-of-Terror-esque.

113 K St., 916-443-2181
evangelines.com

96

BE RED CARPET WORTHY
EVERY DAY AT R. DOUGLAS

You see them on the talk shows. You see them on the red carpet. You see them in the movies. And you marvel at how sharp their clothes look, unlike your own flat-front slightly wrinkled permanent press khakis. Their secret (or at least one of them)? Could be R. Douglas Custom Clothier, where celebrities, governors, politicians, and others world-wide turn for their wardrobe. And you can dress to impress too! If you are new to the exploration of such accoutrements, no need to worry. They'll guide you through the process, in an exploration of fabric compositions, weights, textures, and patterns, to meet your occasion, business setting, and budget. ZZ Top sang about a "Sharp Dressed Man," and you can live it!

1020 Twelfth St., Ste. 112, 916-438-9455
rdouglas.net/locations/sacramento

HAVE THE BEST
CORN DOG EVER

They really have the biggest and best corn dog that you will ever eat. They're available year-round, and that's only one reason to make the twenty-mile drive to Denio's Farmers Market & Swap Meet. Founded in 1947 by Jim and Marilee Denio as Denio's Roseville Farmers Market, by the 1960s Denio's had become and remains the largest, cleanest, and most efficiently run farmers market, auction, and bazaar in California. From fresh corn to a reasonably priced one hundred terabyte external hard drive, you'll likely find it here. You'll find the bargains easily, but your biggest challenge will be deciding between the aforementioned corn dog and the Jimboy's taco. My tip: stay long enough to have both.

1551 Vineyard Rd., Roseville, 916-782-2704
deniosmarket.com

98

STEP INTO
THE STAGE NINE WAYBACK MACHINE

Take a slight step backward in time and plan to spend some time browsing, marveling, remembering, savoring, gawking, tasting, playing, and being a kid again! Stage Nine Family of Specialty Retail Stores inhabits what was once an old sound stage and movie production studio, and is now a wonderland of everything in pop culture, movies, television, nostalgia, animation, clothing, vintage confections, and thousands of other unique memorabilia items. Not to mention being one of California's premier animation art and movie studio galleries. The Stage Nine Entertainment Store, G. Willikers! Toy Emporium, the Vault, the Old Fashioned Candy and Confectionery Store, and California Clothiers are all under one roof for your wayback machine riding pleasure. You don't just pop in and pop out again. You'll be back for more Wax Lips and Atomic Fireballs!

102 K St., 916-447-3623
stagenine.com

PREPARE
FOR THE ZOMBIE APOCALYPSE AT THE SACRAMENTO ANTIQUE FAIRE

I'm only saying that because a Cold War–era bomb shelter survival kit was my big find at the Sacramento Antique Faire, one of the five largest antique vendor meet-ups in California. An outdoor antiques and collectibles marketplace is held the second Sunday of every month, with three hundred vendors from all over the West Coast selling antique and vintage goods, such as furniture, clothing, jewelry, military items (e.g. Cold War–era bomb shelter survival kits), garden items, architectural salvage, lighting, and much more. Some of the area's best food trucks and vendors are also on hand, as you'll need to carb-load for the apocalypse!

2100 X St., 916-600-9770
sacantiquefaire.com

TIP

Always check the website first before you go.
This is a weather-permitting open air event.

100

BE COOL
IN THE ICE BLOCKS

Sacramento's historic R Street Corridor, having evolved from a once neglected strip of gritty warehouses, is now the city's coolest neighborhood! Known as the Ice Blocks, it pays tribute to its heritage as a cold-storage facility. A mixture of cool and eclectic shops serve visiting customers and local residents and office workers with excellent one-of-a-kind fashion, state-of-the-game fitness, and world-class food and beverage. And the sidewalks are wide enough for the occasional pop-up concert. An homage to Midtown's rich history, it's an urban edge with a neighborhood vibe at the Ice Blocks—all in one city block!

1715 R St., 916-638-2400
iceblocksmidtown.com

TIP

Don't miss Milk Money Handmade Ice Cream & Donut Shop. Their name says it all. The best gourmet donut experience you will ever have!

SUGGESTED ITINERARIES

LET'S EAT!

DESSERTS

ON TAP

ADVENTURE LOVERS

DATE NIGHT

• •

SPORTS & GAME FANS

MUSIC FANS

FUN WITH THE KIDS

LET'S DO IT OUTSIDE

OFF THE BEATEN PATH

INDEX